THE USE OF VEGETABLE DYES

VIOLETTA THURSTAN

DRYAD PRESS LTD
LONDON

Fourteenth edition published in 1975
This edition first published 1986
Reprinted 1988

ISBN 0 8521 9654 7

Printed by
Biddles Ltd, Guildford
for the publishers
Dryad Press Ltd
8 Cavendish Square, London W1M 0AJ

Contents

Introduction

Is this "vegetable dyeing" that we are hearing so much about less trouble than chemical dyeing?

No, it is more trouble.

Is it, then, quicker?

No, it takes much longer.

Is it a faster dye?

No, a really fast chemical dye cannot be surpassed by any vegetable dye.

Is it cheaper?

No, the cheap chemical dyes in packets cost only a few pence.

Why, then, should anyone trouble to learn how to use vegetable dye?

Because of the beauty of its results. Those who use it claim that no chemical dye has that lustre, that under-glow of rich colour, that delicious aromatic smell, that soft light and shadow that give so much pleasure to the eye. These colours are *alive* as all beauty is alive; and that is why we would like every craftworker in general, and every weaver and embroiderer in particular, to learn something of vegetable dyeing.

KEY TO RECIPES FOR COLOURS

BRITISH DYE PLANTS (The numbers refer to recipes on pages 18 to 26.)			FOREIGN DYESTUFFS (Recipe numbers for pages 35 to 45.)
	YELLOWS		**YELLOWS**
Alder, spp.	Dog's Mercury, 10.	Pear, 28.	*Flavine, 19.
Apple, 2.	*Dyer's Greenwood, 11.	Pine Cones, 29.	*Fustic, 19, 21.
Ash, 2.	_Dwarf Birch._	_Plum Leaves._	*Kutch, _p._ 32.
*Barberry, 1.	Fig Leaves 12	_Poplar ,,_	*Persian Berries, 18, 20.
Bedstraw, 3.	*Golden Rod, 14.	Privet, 30.	Quercitron Bark, _p._ 33.
*Birch Bark, 4.	*Gorse, 15.	*Ragwort, 31.	*Weld, 22.
Bog Asphodel.	*Heather, 16.	_Tansy, spp._	
Bog Myrtle.	St. John's Wort, 18.	*Weld, 35.	
*Bracken, 6.	*Lichen, _p._ 28.		
Broom, 7.	*Ling, 21.	Yellowwort, 37.	
Camomile, 9.	Marigold, 23.		
	GREENS		**GREENS**
Alchemilla.	Elder, 13.	Privet, 30.	*Fustic, 24.
Alder.	_Horse Tail (Equisetum)._	Reeds, 32.	*Indigo, etc., 24, 25.
Bearberries.		_Sorrel, spp._	
*Bracken, 6.	_Lily of Valley._	_Tamarisk, spp._	
Buckthorn, 8.	*Ling, 21.	_Tansy, spp._	
	BROWNS		**BROWNS**
*Birch Bark, 4.	Juniper, 19.	Onion Skins, 27,	*Fustic, 27.
Bird Cherry, 2.	Larch, 20.	Pine Cones, 29	*Kutch, 28.
Blackberry, 5.	*Lichen, _p._ 28.	Sloe, 33.	*Logwood, 27.
Buckthorn, 8.	Oak, 26.	*Walnut, 34.	*Madder, 26.
Hop, spp.			_Myrobalans, spp._
			Sumach, _p._ 33.
			Valonia Acorns.
	BLACK		**BLACK**
Blackberry, 5.	Elder, 13.	Meadow Sweet, 24.	*Logwood, 30.
Dock Root.	Iris, 17.	*Walnut, 34.	
	REDS		**REDS**
Alkanet.		*Madder, 22.	*Cochineal, 1, 2, 3, 5, 6, 7, 8.
Bedstraw, 3.	St. John's Wort, 18.	_Sorrel, spp_	_*Kermes, spp._
Blackberry, 5.	*Lichen, p. 28.		*Madder, 9, 10,
			Red Woods.
	BLUES		**BLUES AND GREYS**
Bearberries, spp.	_Cornflower, spp._	Sloe, 33.	*Indigo, 11, 12, 13.
Blackberry, 5.	_Devil's Bit._	Whortleberry, 36.	*Logwood, 14, 15, 16.
Buckthorn, 8.	Dog's Mercury, 10.	_Woad, spp._	
Carrot, spp.			
	ORANGE		**ORANGE**
*Lichen, _p._ 28.	Onion Skins, 27	*Weld, 35.	*Flavine, _p._ 31.
			*Fustic, 23.
			*Madder, 23.
			Turmeric, _p._ 34.
	PURPLES		**PURPLES**
*Birch Bark, 4.	_Damson, spp._	_Potentilla, spp._	*Cochineal, 4.
Bryony, spp.	Elderberries, 13.		Cudbear, _p._ 29.
			*Logwood, 17.
			Orchil, _p._ 29.

* An asterisk indicates the most important plants.

No recipes are given for the dye plants and dyestuffs shown in italic. They have been included by the author as, although not being very practicable for various reasons, dyes for the colours given may be obtained from them.

The Dye-House

WHERE it is possible, it is desirable to keep a special room as a dye-house, even if it is only a small pantry or a tool-shed. A sink fitted with hot and cold water is the greatest comfort and saves much time and trouble. If the water is hard, it is worth any amount of trouble to collect rain-water for the actual dyeing and for the washing of wool.

There should be a large, strong table under the window, and one wall should be fitted up with three rows of shelves. The other necessaries are a set of weights and scales, a pestle and mortar, a water thermometer, a gallon-measure glass, some basins, two or more large aluminium pots such as are used for jam making, large enamel saucepans or galvanised iron vessels for dyeing in, an enamel slop pail, and two or three basins of enamel or pottery. A chopping-board and sharp knife are very useful.

For the actual dyeing, a small copper with a place for the fire underneath, and a tap at the bottom so that it can easily be emptied, is good. Another easy method of heating the copper is to have a large gas-ring on the floor, and the copper supported by bricks on each side. Otherwise, a small kitchen range, an oil-stove or an ordinary gas-ring may have to suffice. (Amateur dyers will find themselves unpopular if they heat dye-pots over the kitchen fire or mix dye in the bath). In the table drawer should be kept ordinary labels, poison labels, note-book and pencil, and a pair of scissors. Some smooth wooden sticks for stirring the dye and for lifting skeins of wool out of boiling liquor should be kept handy. These will want renewing frequently, as the sticks become impregnated with dye and may stain a light-coloured skein of wool very badly. Glass rods are better, but are somewhat expensive.

Those who object to their hands and nails being continually stained with dye should provide themselves with a pair of rubber gloves.

The Shelves

The top shelf should be well out of children's reach, as here the mordants (page 9), some of which are poisonous, should be kept. All mordants should be very carefully labelled, and poisonous ones should have a special POISON label.

On the middle shelf should be arranged tins or boxes of dyestuffs. Bulky dyestuffs, such as dried weld or lichens, should be kept in large bags or sacks, and hung on hooks attached to the wall.

On the lower shelf the pots and pans may be placed. These must be kept scrupulously clean; no good dye can possibly come out of a dirty vessel.

Practical Hints

1. Some dyes will form a thick crusted rim all round the pan. This may be cleaned off with Vim, sand and soap, or a little wood ash.

2. No vessel that has been used for indigo should ever be used for anything else; it should be reserved for indigo dyeing only.

3. A large pot, for the boiling with soap and water after dyeing which some colours require, should also be kept separate and never used for dyeing. A large galvanised-iron pot with a lid, very suitable for this purpose, may be bought at an ironmonger's.

Mordanting and Mordants

THERE are two classes of dyes:

1. *Non-mordant* (sometimes called substantive dyes), which impart their colour direct to the wool or other material without any preliminary preparation. The lichen dyes are the most important in this section.

2. *Mordant dyes* (sometimes called adjective dyes), in which the fibre to be dyed has to receive special preparation before it can absorb the colour. The process of preparation is called mordanting.

Mordanting is quite as important as dyeing: in fact, the success of the dyeing rests chiefly on the mordanting. An unevenly mordanted skein of wool can never be an evenly dyed skein. Wool is easy to mordant, as the fibres are porous. Silk is tiresome to do. "Silk boiled is silk spoiled" once the first casing of gum is off, and it has to be steeped for a long time in a tepid or cold mordant solution.

Cotton and linen are both difficult to do well. The fibres are very tough and strong and it is difficult to get the mordant to penetrate.

Different mordants produce different shades of colour; for example, a tin mordant usually brightens a colour, whilst an iron mordant generally darkens it.

There are many different mordants, but the four most useful to a beginner are:

(1) Alum. (2) Tin. (3) Chrome. (4) Iron.

(1) Alum Mordant

Alum (potassium aluminium sulphate) is the most commonly used of all the mordants, and was known to and employed by dyers from the most ancient times. It is generally used in combination with cream of tartar, as this brightens and evens the colour.

(*a*) *Wool* mordanted with alum. Most dye-books give ¼ lb. alum as the proportion necessary for mordanting 1 lb. wool.

This is satisfactory for rather coarse or strong wool, but for fine, delicate wool or embroidery wool it is too much, as it tends to make the wool sticky, and for this kind of wool 3 oz. alum to 1 lb. wool is a better proportion.

Recipe. 3 oz. to 4 oz. alum.
1 oz. cream of tartar.
1 lb. wool.
Large pot cold water.

Method. Dissolve the alum and cream of tartar, and add it to the pot of water. Put the pot on the fire and stir well. As the water begins to get warm, enter the wool and bring the temperature up gradually till it reaches boiling-point. At this point remove the pot to a cooler place on the stove and let it simmer; one hour for coarse, strong wool and about three-quarters of an hour for tender wool. The mordanting is then finished. Lift the wool out of the pot with a stick and let it drain a moment. Then squeeze the excess of water gently out of it, but do not wring or wash it. The wool may be dyed immediately, but it is better left for a day or two. It may be put into a linen bag so that it will remain damp. In some cases, especially in making reds, the mordanting and dyeing may be done in the same pot, but with this exception, the shades are not as bright as where the mordanting and dyeing are done separately.

(*b*) *Silk* mordanted with alum. Raw silk is covered with a yellow, sticky gum which has to be removed before it can take the dye. In order to do this, the skeins are first sewn up in a muslin bag, and then immersed in a hot soap solution ($\frac{1}{2}$ lb. soap to 1 lb. silk). It should then be brought up to the boil and kept just under boiling-point for an hour. It is then taken out of the bags and the soap washed out and is then ready for mordanting. If silk is bought from a firm, this process is generally already done.

The greatest care is needed in mordanting silk, as it very easily loses its lustre. Before mordanting it should be gently washed in tepid water.

Recipe. 1 lb. silk.
4 oz. alum.
1 oz. cream of tartar.
Pot tepid water.

Method. Dissolve the alum and cream of tartar and add them to the water. Enter the silk, and bring the water very slowly up to 100°F. Then take off the pot and allow the silk to get cold in it. Let it remain steeping in this solution for twelve or fifteen hours. The silk should be dyed before it gets dry.

(*c*) *Cotton and linen* mordanted with alum. There are several methods of preparing these hard, tough fibres to receive colour.

Here is one method:

(1) *Boiling*. Boil for at least an hour in water with a little soda and soap in it. This is to cleanse it thoroughly. After boiling, it is left steeping in the solution for twenty-four hours. (Some of the old French dyers recommend its being boiled in "sour" water, i.e. water with chopped sorrel in it, or very weak sulphuric acid).

(2) *Galling*. Steep the cotton or linen in a strong astringent solution such as tannic acid, 1 oz. to 1 lb. Bring it up to boiling-point and let it simmer for half an hour. Then take the pot off the fire and let the cotton get cold in the solution.

(3) *Remove* from galling solution after several hours' steeping and wash.

(4) *Aluming*. This process should be done as for wool, but the cotton should be left soaking in the alum solution for several hours.

(2) Tin Mordant

Tin, usually bought as crystals of tin, muriate of tin, or stannous chloride, is chiefly used when very bright shades of red and yellow are wanted for wool and silk. It is sometimes used as a mordant, sometimes only put into the dye-bath towards the end of dyeing so as to brighten the colour*. Tin should always be carefully dissolved before putting into a pot made of galvanised iron, as it destroys the surface.

½ oz. tin crystals and 2 oz. cream of tartar are used to 1 lb. wool.

Process as for alum mordanting.

This mordant is not a suitable one for linen and cotton, but some tin crystals may be added to the alum mordant if very bright colours are wanted.

(3) Chrome Mordant

Bichromate of potash is the preparation of chromium generally used.

* It is almost always used with cream of tartar, and sometimes in combination with oxalic acid and cream of tartar. The cream of tartar should be dissolved in the water before putting in the tin.

This is a very useful mordant, as it gives wool a very soft and silky feel. A lid should be kept on the pot of bichromate mordant, as it is very sensitive to light, and the dye may be uneven if this is not done. For the same reason wool should not be exposed to light after mordanting with chrome. It should be washed after mordanting, and if it is not going to be used for some time, it should be put in a closed drawer or linen bag.

$\frac{1}{4}$ to $\frac{1}{2}$ oz. bichromate of potash is used to 1 lb. wool.

Process as for mordanting with alum.

(4) Iron Mordant

Ferrous sulphate, or copperas.

Iron, or copperas, is rather a difficult mordant to use, as wool mordanted with it is apt to dye unevenly if great care is not taken. Cream of tartar is almost always used in combination with it. The tendency of iron is to darken and dull colours. In the case of the other mordants mentioned, the mordanting precedes the dyeing. With iron, the reverse process is often employed for wool. The wool is boiled with the dye first and the mordant added after.

$\frac{1}{2}$ oz. copperas and 1 oz. cream of tartar are used to 1 lb. wool.

Process. Boil the wool for half an hour in the dye, then take it out of the pot. Dissolve the copperas and cream of tartar, and add them to the dye. When thoroughly mixed, the wool is replaced, and the dyeing continued. This is sometimes called a "saddening process."

Other Mordants

Copper sulphate and chrome alum are two other mordants sometimes used, but beginners are recommended to use the mordants above mentioned until they are more experienced.

Four Points to Remember in Mordanting

1. Too much alum makes the wool sticky.
2. Too much tin makes it harsh and brittle.
3. Too much chrome impairs the colour.
4. Too much iron hardens the wool.

Practical Hints

1. Be sure that your skeins are properly tied before mordanting, otherwise they are sure to come undone, and it may be hours of work getting them wound up again.

2. Be sure, however, that they are not too tightly tied, or it will be impossible for the mordant to penetrate at these points, and the result will be white patches after the dyeing has taken place.

3. Make sure that the mordant is quite dissolved before putting in the wool or other material to be mordanted, or there may be bad stains in the dyeing.

4. Be careful that your pot is big enough for your wool. No successful mordanting can be done in an overcrowded pot.

5. If it is wool that is being mordanted, the dyer should be careful not to stir too much, or the wool will become felted, i.e. the strands will adhere to each other and become shorter. It may be gently turned over with a stick two or three times during the mordanting process.

Dyeing

IT is more accurate to speak of natural dyes than of "vegetable dyes," but people so often speak loosely of "vegetable dyeing" that it has come to mean any dye that is not a chemical one, and it has therefore been used in this book in this sense. Actually natural dyes may be:

Animal, such as *cochineal*, the small dried bodies of the *Coccus cacti*.

Vegetable, such as *weld* or wild mignonette. Nearly all natural dyes are of plant origin.

Mineral, such as *iron rust*, which dyes a beautiful deep red. The sails of fishing-boats in the Mediterranean are still thus dyed, and so are many of the *portières* and sun-blinds in Italy.

Here are two pieces of practical advice for beginners:

1. It is better to begin by dyeing wool, and leave cotton and linen until proficiency has been gained. The fibres of cotton and linen are hard and strong, and they have to be very carefully prepared before they will take dye at all. Wool is softer and more elastic, and is much easier to dye.

2. It is a mistake to try too many "fancy" dyes at first. There are very many plants that will yield a dye, but VERY FEW THAT WILL YIELD A GOOD BRIGHT COLOUR, FAST TO WASHING AND SUNLIGHT. It is better to stick to these few at first until the dyer is skilful enough to try experiments.

Preparation of Wool

Wool must be thoroughly washed before being dyed to remove all fat and dirt. If wool is greasy or dirty, the colour cannot be fast as dirt and grease absorb the dye. The wool should be washed at least twice in warm, soapy water and rinsed afterwards till the water is quite clear. It may be mordanted while still damp.

Method of Dyeing

The dyestuff is usually put into cold water, is brought slowly up to the boil, and allowed to simmer slowly just below boiling-point for a varying period of time before the wool is entered. If the dyestuff is in powder form, such as Flavine or Sumach, great care should be taken to make sure it is properly dissolved and that there are no lumps before the wool is put in, otherwise there will be uneven dyeing.

If the dyestuff is composed of twigs, which might become entangled in the wool, some dyers tie them up in muslin bags. Others strain the liquor off and dye with that.

Some dyestuffs, barks, for instance, require long boiling before they yield a good colour: others are spoilt by this; for instance, nearly all the yellows. They are always dyed at a rather low temperature (140°–150° F.); long boiling dulls and darkens the colour. Prolonged boiling also spoils the bright red tones of madder and tends to make them brown.

Skeins of wool are lifted in and out of the dye liquor with sticks. Care should be used with this; a deeply stained stick may spoil a batch of wool. The dye liquor should penetrate to every part of the wool, but much stirring and moving should be avoided as soon as the wool is in; this is very likely to make it felt, or become matted together. Dye cannot be stirred too much before the wool is in, or too little afterwards. The whole batch may be gently turned over once or twice to ensure even dyeing.

There are three methods of dyeing:

1. The wool is previously mordanted, and then dyed in a separate dye-bath.

2. The mordant and dye are in the same bath. Some reds and yellows do very well with this method.

3. The wool is dyed first, and the colour fixed afterwards. This process is called stuffing, or saddening, and is generally used with such dyes as Kutch, or sometimes Logwood. It tends to darken and dull colours as a rule, but make them extremely fast.

Dyeing continues until the desired shade is reached. It is difficult for a beginner to match shades at first; it should be remembered that wool looks darker in the dye-bath than after it is washed and dried.

It is well to let the wool get cold in the bath before removing. Wool will go on taking up colour after it is removed from the dye-bath, especially if it contains any of the hot liquor. This is sometimes the cause of wool looking very unevenly dyed, even when the greatest care has been taken in the dyeing. Fine wool and loosely spun wool take up much more colour than coarse wool, or than very tightly spun wool, and two wools of different textures may come out looking quite different from the same dye-bath. After the wool is lifted out, the excess dye liquor should be gently squeezed out. It should then be washed. Running water is of course an ideal way, but this is very rarely possible. It must be rinsed again and again in clear water, until there is no colour coming away. Then, for certain colours, especially reds and yellows, a hot soap bath is a great improvement, as it brightens and sets the colour. The wool is then dried.

Storing of Wool

The possibility of moths getting into the wool must never be forgotten. For this reason, wool should always be easily accessible and never shut up. It is a good plan to keep it hung up in linen bags, or it may be kept on shelves made of wire-netting. It should often be looked at and aired.

Collection of Plants

ALL parts of plants are used for dyeing—the roots, stalks, twigs, leaves, flowers, seeds, berries, and the bark.

Plants which are to be used for dyeing must be collected when they are young and vigorous. Plants which have run to seed are no good.

Roots are generally best collected in autumn; leaves just as they are coming into full growth; bark, *if resinous*, should be collected in spring, otherwise it is best collected in autumn; berries and seeds as soon as they are ripe. Lichens are best collected in winter or after long periods of rain, as they can be then scraped off more easily.

Many plants can be used either fresh or dried, but on the whole the dye is stronger, and the colour more vivid, when they are fresh. Flowers yield their dye easily, but the colour loses brilliancy if boiled too long. Lichens, berries, barks, and roots can be used dried, but great care should be taken with their storage; if they are at all damp when stored, they become mouldy and worthless. Leaves should either be used at once when picked or carefully dried. They may be dried out of doors in the day, and brought in and laid on newspapers on the floor at night.

The following is a list of the chief dye plants found in Great Britain. An asterisk is placed in front of the most important of these. It is not pretended that each of these is a permanent and first-class dye plant, but many people find great interest in collecting and experimenting with their local plants. There is often not enough of a certain plant for the great dyers to trouble with, but the humble dyer who goes on in his or her small way can find great worth in many of these. Also every kind of plant from which a dye is obtained is a product of geographic environment, the quality of which depends on climate, soil, water, aspect, and other conditions. Thus a plant in the north of England may produce a better dye than the same plant in the south, and vice versa. The same plant may give a different shade of colour if gathered at different periods of the year.

British Dye Plants and Recipes

1. *Barberry (*Berberis vulgaris*)

A shrub with yellow flowers and later on small red berries. It is occasionally found in hedges or open woods, but it is probably not a truly wild plant. The stem or root can be used fresh or dried, and produces a yellow dye. Alum is the common mordant, but this is a substantive dye, and can be used equally well without a mordant. A tin mordant (page 11) gives a still deeper colour. This dye is used chiefly for silk.

2. Bark of Trees: Apple (*Pyrus malus*), Ash (*Fraxinus excelsior*), Bird Cherry (*Prunus padus*)

The bark is used either fresh or dried.

Mordant. 4 oz. alum, 2 oz. cream of tartar.

Process The bark is chopped up small and boiled for two hours or longer, and then the mordanted wool is put in and dyed until the required depth of colour is obtained.

Colour. Apple and ash give varying shades of dull yellow to deep gold according to the length of time it is boiled. Bird cherry gives a light chocolate colour if boiled for a long time. If combined with ½ oz. madder to 1 lb. wool, a brownish pink can be obtained.

3. Bedstraw (*Galium boreale*)

A plant common on banks, roadsides, and fields. The stem ends in a cluster of very numerous small yellow flowers. It is interesting as being one of the very few native plants that will produce red. The roots are used for dyeing, 1 lb. to 1 lb. of wool. If the yarn is mordanted with alum and cream of tartar, a yellowish red is obtained; if mordanted with chrome, a more crimson red. The stem and tops are sometimes used as a dye in Ireland; with alum they give a yellow dye.

* The most important plants are indicated by an asterisk.

4. ★Birch (*Betula alba*)

A common tree all over Great Britain.
The leaves and bark are not much used in England, but are in Scandinavia.

(*a*) *Leaves* These may be used fresh or dried. If fresh, 2 lb. leaves to 1 lb. yarn; if dried, double the quantity is necessary. Mordanted with alum, a good yellow is obtained.

(*b*) *Bark* This will give a reddish brown. If mordanted with iron, it tends towards purple. When mordanted with alum, a dull yellow to deep gold is obtained (see recipe No. 2).

5. Blackberry (*Rubus fruticosus*)

(*a*) The young green shoots give an almost black colour if mordanted with iron (copperas) ½ oz. copperas, 1 oz. cream of tartar. (page 12).

(*b*) *Berries.*

Mordant 4 oz. alum, 2 oz. cream of tartar, and 1 oz. common salt to 1 lb. wool.
1 lb. berries, or more if a deep shade is required.

Process The berries are crushed, put into cold water, brought up to the boil, and the mordanted wool put in.

Colour Bluish grey for wool. Slate-blue for silk.

An alum mordant will give a brownish grey to wool. Silk mordanted in the same way but with the addition of cream of tartar will be dyed a pretty rose colour.

6. ★Bracken (*Pteris aquilina*)

The young shoots and root picked in early June will give a good yellow or yellowish green. Soak in cold water for an hour, bring slowly to the boil and leave to simmer for 2 hours. Then wool, previously mordanted with alum and cream of tartar, is entered, and left for about two hours to get cold in the mordant. A pretty green is obtained if the yellow wool is dyed afterwards in a pot of light indigo and left until the desired shade is obtained. In the Highlands, the root of the bracken is used for producing the dark yellow in some tartans.

7. Broom (*Cytisus scoparius*)

Found on dry hilly wastes and bushy places. Common in England, Ireland, and the greater part of Scotland. It is best collected at end of April. Gives a bright yellow dye when mordanted with alum and cream of tartar (page 10). An old French dye-book says: 'Yellow is amongst us prepared with dyer's weed (weld) and finished with broom.'

1 lb. broom to 1 lb. wool is the quantity required.

8. Buckthorn (*Rhamnus catharticus*)

A thorny bush with berries that are red at first and turn black later on.

(*a*) *Bark*. This is chopped up and boiled for three hours, and gives a strong, brownish yellow with alum (page 9) and a deep brown with an iron mordant (page 12). With a little indigo it gives a deep olive-green.

(*b*) *Berries*.

Mordant 4 oz. alum and 2 oz. cream of tartar to 1 lb. wool. 1 lb. berries.

Process The berries should be well bruised before use.

Colour Grey-blue.

9. Camomile (*Anthemis tinctoria*)

Is found chiefly in eastern England. The flowers are daisy-like, with bright yellow rays, and flower in the late summer. The heads may be collected and dried for later use.

Mordant 4 oz. alum and 2 oz. cream of tartar to 1 lb. wool. 1 lb. flower heads.

Process The flowers are put into cold water, brought up to the boil, and simmered for one hour. Then the mordanted wool is entered and boiled again for another hour.

Colour A good bright yellow.

10. Dog's Mercury (*Mercurialis perennis*)

Found in woods and shady places almost everywhere in England and parts of Scotland. Very rare in Ireland. Flowers in early spring. It is best collected in March or April.

Mordant 4 oz. to 1 lb. wool.

Dye 2 lb. of the plant to 1 lb. wool.

Process The plant should be chopped up, put into a cold

bath, and brought gradually up to the boil. The mordanted wool is then entered and simmered until the desired depth of colour is obtained.

Colour The first colour is yellow. If boiling is prolonged, it becomes bluish.

11. *Dyer's Greenwood or Dyer's Broom (*Genista tinctoria*)

Found in Southern England on banks and waste places and flowering in early summer. It should be gathered in June, and may be dried for winter use. It is generally used with an alum and cream of tartar mordant, and gives a strong, bright yellow. It should be well chopped before use. 1 lb. to 1 lb. wool is generally used. Formerly the dyed wool was given an indigo bath to make it green, hence its name.

12. Fig Leaves

These should be collected while young and fresh and well chopped and bruised before use. With alum and cream of tartar mordant, a pale lemon yellow dye is produced with a delicious smell that the dye retains for a long time. 1 lb. leaves to 1 lb. wool, or more if a deeper colour is desired.

13. Elder (*Sambucus nigra*)

A large shrub very common all over England.

The leaves give a green colour with alum mordant (page 9). The berries give a blue-lilac colour with alum mordant and salt, a violet colour with alum mordant only. The bark gives a black colour with iron mordant (page 12).

In each case 1 lb. to 1 lb. wool.

14. *Golden Rod (*solidago spp.*)

A tall perennial with long flower heads made up of numerous small yellow flowerets. Abundant in Great Britain, especially on chalky soil. It should be picked just as the flower is coming into bloom.

Mordant Bichromate of potash, 2 oz. cream of tartar (page 12) to 1 lb. wool.

Quantity 1 lb.

Process The plant and flower heads should be chopped into

small pieces and put in a pot of cold water. It should be brought slowly up to the boil and simmered for two or three hours, and then allowed to grow cold. The next day heated up again to just below boiling-point, and the mordanted yarn entered and allowed to simmer until the required depth of colour is obtained.

It is suitable for wool, silk, and cotton.

Colour Golden yellow. Alum may be used as a mordant instead of chrome, and the colour is then lemon-yellow.

15. *GORSE (*Ulex europæus*)

The bark, the flowers, and the young shoots can be used. They give a yellow colour. 'Whinbark' was much used in dyeing the Highland tartans.

16. *HEATHER (*Erica Valgaris*)

Ling is the most satisfactory of the heather family for dyeing, but all of them make a yellow dye. (See Ling, page 23.)

17. IRIS (*Iris pseudacorus*)

This is the common yellow flag of our marshes and boggy fields. The root yields a black colour to wool previously mordanted with alum (page 9).

18. ST. JOHN'S WORT (*Hypericum perforatum*)

A common creeping plant with gold-yellow flower. It can be used with different mordants. The tops mordanted with alum, give a yellow or yellow-red colour. The flower heads, mordanted with tin, give a reddish colour.

19. JUNIPER (*Juniperus communis*)

Found on rather dry, barren hills, is commoner in the north of England than in the south. The berries, which take two years to ripen, are used for dyeing. They may be used either fresh or dried. The bark and twigs also yield a dye.

Mordant 4 oz. alum, 1 oz. cream of tartar, copper sulphate.
Dye 1 lb. berries.

Process The berries should be crushed and boiled for two hours mordanted with alum and cream of tartar to give a pretty olive brown. The twigs mordanted in the same way and chopped fine and added to the liquid give a light purplish brown. A darker shade can be obtained if 1 oz. copper sulphate is added to the mordant.

20. Larch (*Pinus Larix*)

The needles collected in autumn give a brown dye to wool previously mordanted with alum (page 9).

21. *Ling (*Calluna vulgaris*)

Common all over Great Britain, especially in moorland and mountain districts. If ling is wanted for winter use, the tips should be picked just before they come into flower. If it is to be used fresh, it can be gathered as long as the flower is in bloom.

Mordant 4 oz. alum, 2 oz. cream of tartar to 1 lb. of wool.

Dye 2 lb. ling tips.

Process The tips should be put into a pot of cold water, brought gradually to the boil, allowed to simmer three or four hours, and then the pot is taken off and allowed to grow cold. Next day the liquor is strained off, and the wool entered and boiled in it until the required depth of colour is reached.

Colour. A good olive-yellow. If some gall apples are added and some iron mordant put in towards the end of dyeing (page 12), a moss-green is obtained.

22. *Madder (*Rubia peregrina*)

This must not be confused with Dyer's Madder (*Rubia Tinctoria*). The latter, which is extensively grown in southern Europe for the beautiful red dye that is obtained from its roots, does not grow wild in England. A rose dye, pinker than Dyer's Madder, is obtained from the roots of the *Rubia Peregrina* found at the edge of woods in the west of England.

The dye is prepared in the same way as *Rubia Tinctoria* (page 33).

23. Marigold (*Caltha palustris*)

Found everywhere in Great Britain. The yellow flower head yields a yellow dye. Alum and cream of tartar mordant.

24. Meadow Sweet (*Spiræa ulmaria*)

The roots of this plant give a black colour. This was used in the Highlands for dyeing the tartans. It is best collected in July.

25. Mignonette

See Weld (page 26).

26. Oak (*Quercus Robur, spp.*)

A decoction of the bark will give a good brown to wool previously mordanted with alum (page 9).

1 lb. bark to 1 lb. wool.

27. Onion Skins (*Allium cepa*)

The outer skins are used. They should be boiled for about two hours, then the yarn, previously mordanted with alum, entered, and boiled for an hour. A golden brown is obtained. The smell soon goes off if the yarn is hung out in the open air. A tin mordant instead of alum gives a more orange colour. This is not a very fast dye.

28. Pear (*Pyrus communis*)

Mordant 4 oz. alum, 1 oz. cream of tartar, ½ oz. powdered chalk to 1 lb. wool.

Dye 1 lb. leaves.

Process The wool is mordanted, and then pear leaves well bruised, can be put into the same water and gradually brought to the boil, then simmered gently till the required depth of colour is reached.

Colour Dull yellow.

29. Pine Cones (*Pinus spp.*)

Mordant 4 oz. alum to 1 lb. wool.

Dye 1½ lb. cones.

Process The cones should be broken up small and boiled for three or four hours. The mordanted yarn can then be entered and boiled until the required shade is reached.

Colour Reddish yellow. If an iron mordant (page 12) is added towards the end of dyeing, a darkish brown will be the result.

30. Privet (*Ligustrum vulgare*)

Very common all over Great Britain. The leaves give a yellow colour to yarn mordanted with alum (page 9), the berries a bluish green. 1 lb. berries to 1 lb. wool. The berries should be well bruised before use.

31. *Ragwort (*Senecio jacobæa*)

Very common plant all over Great Britain, especially on roadsides and waste places. It has large yellow flower heads which yield a yellow colour with alum mordant (page 9). It is prepared in the same way as Golden Rod (page 21).

32. Reeds (*Phragmites spp.*)

The pinkish flower heads are chopped up small and boiled very slowly for two hours and then allowed to get cold. The next day the yarn can be boiled in this liquor. It is specially used for linen and cotton yarn, imparting a green colour to them.

These must be gathered very young; old or dried up reeds give very little colour.

Mordant 4 oz. alum, 1 oz. cream of tartar.

Dye 2 lb. twigs.

Process As ling (page 23).

Colour Light green to wool previously mordanted with alum.

33. Sloe (*Prunus spinosa*)

This is the fruit of the Blackthorn, a purplish-blue berry with a silver bloom. On boiling without any mordant it gives a rosy colour. This turns afterwards to slate-blue if washed with soap. An alum mordant makes the colour faster. It is a better dye for silk than for wool. 1 lb. well-bruised berries to 1 lb. wool.

The bark gives a good red-brown. 2 lb. bark to 1 lb. wool.

34. *Walnut (*Juglans regia*)

The shells and husks are both used. The walnuts are collected when ripe and put into a cask and covered with water. Store them from light. They give a substantive dye, so mordant is not required. Some dyers use alum mordant but this yellows the dyes a little, (page 9). The longer the wool is kept in this solution, the deeper brown it will become, but delicate wool is not suitable for a walnut dye as it makes it hard and brittle. The husks should be boiled up for $\frac{1}{2}$ hour or more and then allowed to cool, the wool is then entered, and it is boiled up again until the desired tone is obtained. It is used to produce a good black, in combination with other dyes, especially indigo and logwood.

35. *Weld or Wild Mignonette (*Reseda luteola*)

Grows in waste places, especially sandy places. Has a habit of disappearing and then reappearing after a few years. It produces the best and most permanent of all the vegetable dyes. It can be used either fresh or dry. Care must be taken to collect it before it seeds, as the colour is then very poor.

Mordant. An alum mordant (page 9) gives a lemon-yellow, a chrome mordant (page 11) a golden yellow, a tin mordant (page 11) a yellow-orange, an iron mordant (page 12) an olive-yellow. The colour is richer if a little powdered chalk, 1 oz. to 1 lb., is added to the dye-bath. The whole plant (except root) is used.

Process. It is chopped up (some people put it in a muslin bag), placed in a pot of cold water, brought to the boil, and simmered for three hours. The wool is then entered.

Colour. Yellow.

Besides dyeing wool, it produces an excellent yellow for silk, mordanted as for wool.

36. Whortleberry (*Vaccinium myrtillus*)

Common in north and west England and all over Scotland, especially on moorlands and in open woods. It has a small purple-blue berry that gives a bluish dye. It is a substantive dye and therefore does not need a mordant, though one is sometimes used. It is used sometimes to 'bottom' indigo, and in the Highlands with alum to give a purplish blue. It is also used with nut galls to give a dark brown. 1 lb. well-bruised berries to 1 lb. wool is required.

37. Yellowwort (*Chlora perfoliata*)

Found only in southern half of England on waste land and dry pastures. Gives a yellow dye to wool mordanted with alum (page 9).

Lichen Dyes

In the 16th and 17th centuries new geographical discoveries brought about a new era in dyeing. The opening of trade routes to America and the Cape route to India brought many new dyes in reach of European dyers. In Great Britain, owing mainly to French and Flemish influences the use of natural dyes was gradually given up in favour of the new foreign dyes.

An exception to this was the important class of lichen dyes. These are not mentioned in Continental text books, with the exception of Archil, or Orchil (see page 29); but lichens have always been extensively used and still are to some extent by people in the North. In Norway, Sweden, Iceland, Wales, the Shetlands, Orkney, Skye and Northern Ireland, lichens are still used for dyeing wool. Harris, Donegal and Shetland tweeds owe their characteristic smell to the boiling lichen.

In an interesting little book called *Scottish Clans and their Tartans*, many of the colours listed in the different Highland Tartans were obtained from lichens, 'Brown, crimson, dark crimson, purple, two kinds of red, scarlet and yellow' .

Lichen growing on stones gives a better colour than the same lichen growing on trees.

There are between 40 and 50 kinds of lichen which give a dye, but amateur dyers need only concern themselves with a few.

In Norway, Sweden, Iceland, the Shetlands, Orkney, Skye, and western Ireland, lichens are still used for dyeing woollens.

There are between forty and fifty kinds of lichen which give a dye, but beginners in dyeing need concern themselves only with a very few. The lichens are substantive dyes, and require no mordant, though some dyers think that a little acetic acid brings out the colour.

Two Methods of Dyeing with Lichens

1. Put the lichen into a large pot and fill up to the top with cold water. About 1 lb. lichen to 1 lb. wool is required.

Bring this up to the boil very slowly and let it simmer for two or three hours, and then get cold. Next day, put the wool, which should be thoroughly wetted first, into the pot, and boil it all up together until the required depth of colour is obtained. The wool should not be taken out until it is cold. Then wash. The loose lichen shakes off quite easily.

2. A layer of lichen at the bottom of the pot, then a layer of wool, another layer of lichen, and so on until the pot is nearly full. Fill up with cold water and put on the fire to simmer for some hours, till the required depth of colour is reached. It can be taken off at night and put on again next day. The colour will be very fast. Wash well.

Common Dye Lichens

Brown

Parmelia saxatilis This has several names: Crottle, Staneraw, Scrottyie, etc. It is found on stones and rocks, especially near the sea, mainly in Scotland and the Shetland Isles, where it is called stanyraw. This dyes a very good shade of orange-brown. It is generally collected in July and August.

Reddish Brown, or Brown

Parmelia omphalodes This is also called Black Crottle in Scotland, Kenkerig in Wales, and Arcel in Ireland. Found on rocks, especially at rather high altitudes, on Dartmoor, Bodmin Moor, Welsh mountains, Scottish highlands, and the west of Ireland. It yields a very good, warm, dark brown or reddish brown. It is this lichen that gives the characteristic "Harris Tweed" smell.

Yellow-brown

Parmelia parietina This is a common bright yellow lichen growing on stone walls, the roofs of old barns, etc. It dyes a yellow-brown, or if mordanted first with bichromate of potash, a warm pinkish brown.

Yellow or Yellow-brown

Ramalina scopulorum This is a very common grey lichen growing on old stone walls, especially by the sea. It also grows on trees in damp, dark woods. It is best gathered in winter or after a heavy fall of rain.

Yellow for Linen

Peltigera canina This is a large, flat lichen growing on rocks, especially in woods. Mordant the linen first with alum, then boil with the lichen for three or four hours, and allow it to grow cold in the dye liquor.

Orange

Lobaria pulmonaria This is also called Oak Lung, Lungwort, Oak Rag. It is found on trees in England, Scotland, and Northern Ireland. It dyes wool orange.

Red

Ochrolechia tartarea This grows plentifully on limestone rocks, and has long been used as a dye by the peasants of Wales, the Shetlands, and the Orkneys. It used to be scraped off the rocks with an iron hoop, and then soaked in stale urine to which a little powdered chalk had been added.

Cudbear and Orchil

There are two preparations of lichen that are interesting to the dyer. One is Archil or Orchil, the other Cudbear. Lindsay in the *New Philosophical Journal* says that we may practically regard Archil as the English, Cudbear as the Scottish and Litmus as the Dutch names for the same substance. The name Cudbear is derived from Dr. Cuthbert Gordon who discovered the process of preparing it. Archil is the only lichen dye mentioned in the old Continental books on dyeing. It was a Florentine named Rucelli who introduced the method of making this dye from certain lichens from Asia Minor.

Different lichens are used in different parts for preparing these dyes. Brewster quotes the Lecanora tartarea (now called Ochrolechia tartarea as being one of the chief ingredients). Both these preparations give beautiful shades of red and purple. They are not often used alone as the colours are not very fast, but Cudbear especially gives a beautiful bloom to wool previously dyed with Cochineal.

Neither linen nor cotton takes this dye.

The preparation of these lichens before dyeing is long and tedious, and the beginner may not want to undertake this, but the process is not very difficult if the following conditions are observed.

Preparation with Ochrolechia tartarea (formerly called Lecanora tartarea).

The principle of preparing this dye is by the fermentation of the lichen with ammonia and water.

1. The lichen should be first bruised, and mixed with a little water to form a paste.
2. Then an ammonia mixture should be added gradually, 1 part of ammonia to 2 of water. Ordinary household ammonia may be used.
3. Put into a closed vessel to ferment, and keep in a warm place for about a month. An airing cupboard is a good place if not too hot. The temperature should not exceed 75°.
4. It should be stirred frequently to permit of oxygenation.
5. At the end of the fermentation period, a little powdered lime can be mixed in, enough to make it solid enough to roll into balls or cakes. In Scotland, these balls are hung up in peat until required. When smoked, they can be kept almost indefinitely.

Dyestuffs Imported from Foreign Countries

Cochineal and Kermes

THESE two dyestuffs are animal, not vegetable, in nature, but as they are natural, not synthetic, dyes, and very important ones, they are included here.

★Cochineal

This is prepared from the dried bodies of an insect, the *Coccus cacti*, which lives on the Cactus plants cultivated for this purpose in Mexico, the Canary Islands, and other places. Cochineal gives a different shade of crimson, scarlet, or rose, according to the mordant used.

Alum mordant gives magenta.
Alum and cream of tartar, crimson.
Chrome alum, deep cardinal purple.
Oxalic acid and cream of tartar, deep geranium-red.
Tin crystals and cream of tartar, bright scarlet.
Iron, deep purple-grey.

Kermes

This is used in the same way as cochineal. It makes a very beautiful and permanent dye, produced from the small dried bodies of the insect that burrows into the red berries of the holly oak. This is plentiful in some parts of Eastern Europe, especially in the mountainous regions of Greece (Euboea etc.), but unfortunately very difficult to obtain in the British Isles.

★Flavine

This is a commercial preparation of Quercitron bark. It produces beautiful yellows and oranges with a tin and cream of tartar mordant. A good fast dye.

Fustic Chips

Is prepared from the wood of the *Morus tinctoria*, or dyer's mulberry tree, which grows in Cuba, Jamaica, and Central America. It gives very beautiful yellow shades, which are fairly fast to sunlight and washing. It is chiefly used in dyeing wool, and if dyed on light indigo gives a very good green.

Alum mordant gives lemon-yellow.
Chrome and cream of tartar, old gold.
Tin and cream of tartar, a deep daffodil yellow.
Iron, olive.

Kutch

Kutch, or Catechu, is prepared from the wood of certain acacia trees. It has a special affinity for cottons, and has been used in India for centuries for giving fine shades of brown on cotton material. It comes into the market in dark-brown cubes, which have to be pounded up before they can be used. They should not be allowed to get damp, as Kutch becomes very sticky and is difficult to pound up.

Alum mordant gives yellowish brown.
Tin and cream of tartar, brownish yellow.
Iron, brownish grey.

It is frequently dyed first and mordanted after (saddened).

*Indigo

Indigo is the name given to the colouring matter produced from the plant, the *Indigo-fera tinctoria*, growing in India and other parts of Asia, and Egypt. It reaches the market as a dark-blue powder, insoluble in water. There are two methods of dyeing with indigo: one by indigo extract, a method of producing indigo blue by dissolving it in sulphuric acid, the other by indigo vat. The latter produces more beautiful and more permanent colours than the former, but is very much more troublesome to prepare.

Logwood or Campeachy Wood

This is the heart-wood of *Hæmatoxylin campeachianum*, a tree growing in South America. It arrives on the market as yellowish chips. In olden times the use of this dye was discouraged, because it was considered to be a fugitive dye. But with very careful mordanting, fast colours can now be produced, and it is a most useful dye, used for wool, cotton, and silk.

Alum mordant gives dark slate-blue and purplish blue.
Tin and cream of tartar, purple.
Iron, black.
Bichromate and cream of tartar, deep grey.

This can be obtained in two forms: (1) chips; (2) Logwood paste or extract.

*Madder

Consists of the dried roots of the *Rubia tinctoria*, formerly largely cultivated in France and Holland.

Alum and cream of tartar mordant gives brownish red.
Tin and cream of tartar, bright red.
Chrome mordant, reddish brown.
Iron, purplish brown.

Persian Berries

Sometimes called French berries. These are the dried fruit of a blackthorn growing in Turkey and the Levant. They come on to the market as dry, yellowish berries about as big as a pea, which have to be pounded up in a mortar before being used.

Alum and cream of tartar give a lemon-yellow.
Bichromate and cream of tartar, old gold.
Tin and cream of tartar, deep daffodil yellow.
Iron and cream of tartar, olive-yellow.

Quercitron

This is the inner bark of an oak tree, *Quercus tinctoria*, growing in North America. It produces the same kind of yellow as Fustic (page 32), but it is specially used in combination with indigo for producing bright greens.

Sumach

This is the preparation of the ground-up leaves of the *Rhus coriaria*, a shrub growing in southern Europe. It comes on the market as a yellowish-brown powder. It is used very little for wool, but as it has strong astringent powers, it is very much used in cotton dyeing, giving a yellowish-brown colour.

Turmeric (Korkum)

This is a yellow powder obtained from the ground root of a plant called *Curcuma tinctoria*, found in the East. It is a substantive colour, and without any mordant will give a beautiful orange. Unluckily, it is not fast, and therefore is very little used in England. A little of this added at the end of dyeing with Persian berries gives a beautiful bloom.

*Weld

This used to be imported in large quantities from Normandy and Brittany. (See Wild Mignonette, page 26).

Recipes for the use of Foreign Dyestuffs

Red, Rose, Carmine, Crimson, Scarlet, and Red-Purples

1. Crimson for Wool with Cochineal

1st Method

1 lb. wool mordanted with alum and cream of tartar.
1½ oz. cochineal for a medium shade, 2 oz. cochineal for a deep crimson.
1 dessertspoonful common salt.

Method. Put the cochineal and salt into a pot of tepid water and stir well till they are quite dissolved, then enter the mordanted wool, and bring very slowly up to the boil. Let it simmer, under boiling-point, for an hour, or until the desired depth of colour is reached. The colour is a little deeper and evener if the wool is allowed to grow cold in the dye liquor. Take out the wool, wash, and dry it.

2nd Method

Mordant and dye in the same bath.

1 lb. unmordanted wool.
4 oz. alum.
1½ oz. cream of tartar.
1½ oz. cochineal.

Method. Dissolve the alum and cream of tartar, and when the water is warm enter the wool, and bring it up to the boil and simmer for about twenty minutes. Take out the wool and put in the cochineal. Stir well till quite dissolved, and then re-enter the wool and simmer just under boiling-point for three-quarters of an hour, or until the desired shade is reached.

2. Geranium-red for Wool with Cochineal

By adding a few grains of oxalic acid crystals to the dye-bath mentioned in the first recipe, a bright geranium-red will be obtained.

3. Purple-red for Wool with Cochineal

By substituting a bichromate of potash mordant for the alum mordant in recipe No. 1, a purple-red will be obtained.

4. Violet for Wool with Cochineal

By substituting an iron mordant for the alum mordant in recipe No. 1, a violet will be obtained.

5. Rosy Crimson for Wool with Cochineal

By adding a tablespoonful of Cudbear (see page 29) to the dye-bath in recipe No. 1, a beautiful deep-rose bloom will be given to the wool.

6. Scarlet for Wool with Cochineal

1st Method

1 lb. wool mordanted with tin and cream of tartar.
½ oz. fustic or Persian berries.
2 oz. cochineal.
Tablespoonful common salt.

Method. Mordant wool with tin and cream of tartar. Dye wool slightly yellow in very weak fustic bath. Take out and wash. Prepare dye-bath by adding the cochineal and salt. When thoroughly dissolved, enter the wool, and bring slowly to the boil.

2nd Method

1 lb. unmordanted wool.
1 oz. tin crystals.

1 oz. oxalic acid crystals.
2 oz. cochineal.

Method. Dissolve the tin, oxalic acid, and cochineal in the dye-bath, and bring up to the boil. Add sufficient water to cover the wool. Enter the wool, which should have been previously wetted, and simmer for an hour. Then take out, wash, and dry.

7. Crimson for Cotton with Cochineal

1 lb. galled and mordanted cotton.
1½ oz. cochineal.

(1) Cotton should be galled with sumach, 4 oz. to 1 lb.; i.e. boiled up in it and left to steep for twenty-four hours.

(2) It should then be mordanted for two hours with alum, 4 oz. to 1 lb., left to grow cold in the mordant, and then washed.

(3) Dissolve cochineal in the dye-bath.

(4) Enter the cotton, and simmer it until the required depth of colour is obtained.

8. Crimson for Silk with Cochineal

1 lb. silk mordanted with alum and allowed to steep for twenty-four hours in the mordant bath.
1 oz. cochineal.

Method. Wash the mordanted silk.

Dissolve the cochineal and bring it up slowly to the boil; then let it simmer for thirty minutes, strain off the liquor through a piece of muslin, and let it grow tepid.

Enter the silk when tepid, and increase the temperature very slowly and cautiously (never letting it boil), until the desired depth of colour is obtained. Allow the silk to grow cold in the solution.

9. Red for Wool with Madder

1 lb. wool previously mordanted with alum and cream of tartar.
8 oz. madder.
A little powdered chalk if the water is soft.

Method. The madder may be put to soak the night before; this makes it easier to use, but is not necessary.

It should be put into the dye-bath, and stirred very well as it is brought slowly to the boil, and kept just under boiling-point for about twenty minutes. Then a little more water is added and the wool entered and simmered for an hour. Allow the wool to remain in the dye liquor till cold. Then wash in several waters and pass through a boiling soap-bath. This brightens and improves the colour.

10. Bright Red for Wool with Madder

1 lb. wool mordanted with tin and cream of tartar.
8 oz. madder.

Method. As in No. 9.

Blues, Greys, Lavenders, Blue-Purples

11. Blue for Wool with Indigo

There are two methods of dyeing blue with indigo:

(1) By using indigo extract, which can either be made or be bought ready to use.

(2) By making a hydro-sulphite of soda vat.

Indigo extract is not recommended, as it is a very fugitive dye, but it is a much easier method than the hydro-sulphite vat.

To Make Extract of Indigo Stock Solution

*8 oz. sulphuric acid in a measure glass.
1 oz. ground indigo.
½ oz. precipitated chalk.
Glass or china basin.
Glass stirring-rod.

Method. Put the indigo into the glass basin. Pour in a little sulphuric acid and mix with the glass rod. Add a little chalk. Stir well, and add a little acid, and so on till all is used up. The mixture should finally be put into a stoppered glass jar. It is not

* Sulphuric acid is strong, burning, and highly poisonous. It should never be left where any child could reach it. Even a drop or two on the finger will burn and smart, and if this occurs it should be treated with an alkali, such as common baking-soda.

fit for use for a week, and during that time should be stirred several times and a little more chalk added.

12. To Dye with Indigo Extract

1 lb. unmordanted wool.
½ oz. indigo extract.

Method. Stir the indigo extract into the water of the dye-bath. When warm, enter the wool and bring slowly up to boiling-point, and let it simmer just under boiling-point for three-quarters of an hour.

Take out, wash in several waters, but do not use soap.

If this blue is too green, it can be corrected by adding a little madder to the dye-bath. Some dyers think the colour better if the wool is previously mordanted with alum.

Hydro-sulphite Vat Process

To prepare stock solution:

3 oz. caustic soda.
2 oz. hydro-sulphite soda.
2 oz. powdered indigo.
1 Large jug hot water (about 130°F.).
2 empty jugs or glass measures holding about 1 pint.
1 large pot to hold the stock solution (a 7-lb. jam-pot will do).
Saucepan.
Glass stirring-rod.
Pestle and mortar.
Water thermometer.

Method. (1) Measure out 2 oz. powdered indigo into the mortar. Add a little warm water. Grind the mixture with the pestle until a liquid paste of even consistency has been obtained. Put this in the saucepan.

(2) Take one of the glass measures with 1 pint hot water. Add the caustic soda gradually, stirring with the rod all the time.

(3) Take the other glass measure with 1 pint hot water. Add the hydro-sulphite soda gradually, stirring all the time.

(4) Return to the pot containing the indigo paste. To this add first nearly all of the caustic-soda solution, and then the hydro-sulphite solution. Warm up to temperature 125° F., and leave for half an hour in a warm place.

There should be no guessing at the temperature. The thermometer should be in use during all the processes, if the temperature is too high (140° F. is the limit), the whole vat will be destroyed, and the dyer will have to begin again from the beginning.

If the mixture is rightly prepared, the glass, on taking it out of the solution, should show clear yellow.

There may be two kinds of failure:

(1) Sometimes little dusty spots show upon the yellow-stained glass. This means that some of the indigo is undissolved. There is evidently not enough hydro-sulphite or it is old and has lost some of its strength. In that case, add 2 oz. or 3 oz. of the hydro-sulphite solution left over from the stock glass.

Leave the solution for a time to settle, then test again with glass rod.

(2) The mixture may be thick and milky. That means that there is too much hydro-sulphite. In that case add small quantities of the caustic-soda solution, testing with the glass rod the whole time till it shows clear yellow.

13. To Dye with Hydro-sulphite Vat Indigo

Fill a dye-bath or large bucket with water about 120° F. Add 2 oz. hydro-sulphite solution and 1 oz. salt. Stir well, and leave for twenty minutes. The object of this is to deoxygenate the water.

Add 1 oz. of the indigo stock solution, avoiding making bubbles if possible. If the bath now feels slimy, there is too much caustic soda, and again a little hydro-sulphite of soda solution is added.

The temperature of the dye-bath should be kept between the limits of 120° and 130° F., and should on no account exceed 140°. The wool, which should have been previously thoroughly wetted, should be put in very gently without bubbles, and worked a little before being allowed to dye for half an hour. It should then be taken out, and on exposure to the air should quickly change from a pale yellow into green and finally into a permanent blue. After exposure to the air for half an hour, it may again be put into the dye-bath. If the shade is too light, a little more indigo stock solution may be added, but it is much better to build up a good full shade by a series of dips in a weak vat than to use one or two strong baths. Rubber gloves should be used if possible. When dyed sufficiently, it should be washed. To the first water a teaspoonful of sulphuric acid is sometimes added. This fixes the colour and prevents rubbing.

Finally, the yarn should be put through a bath of boiling soap and water.

14. Grey-blue for Wool with Logwood

1 lb. wool mordanted with alum and cream of tartar.
½ oz. bichromate of potash.
3 oz. logwood.
1 dessertspoonful chalk if water is very soft.

If chips are used, they should be put in a muslin bag before putting in dye-bath. If logwood extract is used (1 oz. equals ½ lb. chips), it should be thoroughly dissolved with the bichromate and chalk before the wool is entered. The dye-bath should be kept just under the boiling-point for three-quarters of an hour. Then the wool is taken out and washed.

15. Grey for Wool with Logwood

1 lb. wool, mordanted with ½ oz. bichromate of potash and 1 oz. cream of tartar.
4 oz. logwood.

Method. After the wool has been in the mordant bath for a quarter of an hour, remove it, and add the logwood chips (previously boiled for twenty minutes). Re-enter the wool, and continue simmering for another half-hour.

16. Grey for Cotton with Logwood

(1) Gall the cotton.
(2) Dye with 4 oz. logwood as in recipe No. 14.
(3) Mordant in a separate bath with bichromate of potash and cream of tartar.

17. Purple for Cotton with Logwood

(1) Gall 1 lb. cotton.
(2) Mordant with iron
(3) Mordant again in another mordant bath with tin.
(4) Dye as in recipe No. 14 with logwood.

Yellow, Gold, and Orange

18. Canary-yellow for Wool with Persian Berries

1 lb. wool mordanted with alum and cream of tartar.
4 oz. Persian berries.

Method. The wool is put into the mordant bath and boiled for 20 minutes, then removed. The berries should be well pounded up, put into the mordant bath, and allowed to simmer well below boiling-point for half an hour. Then the wool is entered again and dyed for three-quarters of an hour to 1 hour according to the depth of colour required.

19. Warm Yellow for Wool with Fustic and Flavine

1 lb. wool mordanted with alum and cream of tartar.
2 oz. fustic chips.
1 oz. flavine.

Method. As in recipe No. 18.

20. Daffodil-yellow for Wool with Persian Berries

1 lb. wool mordanted with bichromate and cream of tartar.
4 oz. Persian berries.

Method. As in recipe No. 18.

21. Yellow for Silk with Fustic

1 lb. silk mordanted with alum.
6 oz. fustic.

Boil up the fustic for half an hour, and then allow the solution to cool. When the temperature is about 140° F., put in the previously mordanted silk and dye it for half an hour.

Steep the silk for an hour in a cool bath in which a teaspoonful of tin has been dissolved.

22. Daffodil-yellow for Wool with Weld

1 lb. wool mordanted with bichromate of potash and cream of tartar.

3 lb. weld.
½ oz. chalk.

Chop the weld up small and put into a pot of cold water with the dissolved chalk. Bring it up to boiling-point. Let it simmer for an hour, and then strain off the stalks. Enter the wool and simmer for three-quarters of an hour.

NOTE.—The weld may be put loosely into a muslin bag.

23. ORANGE FOR WOOL WITH FUSTIC AND MADDER

1 lb. wool mordanted for twenty minutes with tin and cream of tartar.
4 oz. fustic or 4 oz. Persian berries.
½ oz. flavine.
4 oz. madder.

Remove the wool from the mordant bath, and put in the fustic and madder. Boil for half an hour. Add the flavine. Re-enter the wool, and simmer for three-quarters of an hour. Wash and dry.

Green

24. BRIGHT GREEN

(1) The wool should first be dyed blue. The easiest method and one that gives a good, bright green is to dye it a light blue with indigo extract (see recipe No. 12, page 39).

(2) Then mordant in the ordinary way with alum and cream of tartar.

(3) Then yellow with weld, fustic, or Persian berries (see recipes for yellow), until the required tint is obtained. Some dyers prefer to yellow the wool first and dye with blue after.

25. OLIVE-GREEN

(1) Dye wool light blue as in recipe No. 12.
(2) Mordant with bichromate and cream of tartar.
(3) Yellow with bracken buds or flavine.

26. Brown for Wool with Madder

1 lb. wool mordanted with iron and cream of tartar.
8 oz. madder.

(1) Dye as for recipe No. 9.

(2) The wool is sometimes dyed first for half an hour, and the mordant then added, the wool re-entered, and dyeing continued for another half-hour.

27. Tan Colour for Wool with Madder, Fustic, and Logwood

1 lb. wool mordanted with bichromate of potash and cream of tartar.
1 oz. madder.
1 oz. fustic.
½ oz. logwood.

Boil up together the madder, fustic, and logwood for half an hour. Then cool, enter the wool, raise to just under boiling-point, and simmer for three-quarters of an hour.

28. Brown for Cotton with Kutch

Steep the cotton overnight in a decoction of kutch, in the proportion of 4 oz. to 1 lb. The next day, boil this up in a bichromate mordant for one hour.

Wash well and dry.

29. Black for Wool

There are several methods of dyeing wool black. One very good method is to dye first a good dark blue with indigo (see recipe No. 13). Then dye with walnut (page 25).

30. Black from Logwood

1 lb. wool mordanted with ½ oz. bichromate of potash.

8 oz. logwood.

If an intense black is desired, the addition of a few drops of sulphuric acid to the mordant helps.

Logwood alone gives a blue-black.

(1) If a brown-black is desired, some kutch or walnut can be added to the mordant bath.

(2) If dead black is desired, ½ oz. fustic chips can be added to mordant bath. Mordant thoroughly for at least an hour, then take out wool and wash it.

(3) Dissolve the logwood in a bath of warm water, and then enter the wool, bring it up to boil, and dye for at least an hour.

(4) Take out wool and wash thoroughly.

Bibliography

Art of Cleaning, Dyeing, etc. Thomas Love. (Longmans, Green, 1854.)

Art of Dyeing Wool, Silk, and Cotton. Translated from the French. M. Hellot, 1789.

Art of Dyeing. Translated from the German. 1705. Reprint 1913.

Arts and Crafts of Older Spain. Leonard Williams. 1907.

British Flora. Bentham and Hooker. 1924.

Dyeing of Woollen Fabrics. Franklin Beech. 1902.

Dyes and Dyeing. Pellew. (McBride, New York, 1928.)

Egyptian Horticultural Journal, 1924. Articles on Dyeing. Violetta Thurstan.

Elements of the Art of Dyeing. Berthollet. 1791.

Family Dyer and Scourer. Wm. Tucker. 1818.

Farvning med Planter. H. Christensen. 1917.

Hemfärgning med Växtamnen. Beda Larson. 1920.

Manual of Dyeing. James Napier. (Griffin, Glasgow, 1853.)

Notes on Spinning and Dyeing Wool. M. Holding.

Practical Book of Oriental Rugs. Griffin Lewis.

Philosophy of Permanent Colours. Bancroft. 1813.

Scottish Clans and Their Tartans. Anon. (Johnston, Edinburgh.)

Scouring and Dyeing with Vegetable Dye Recipes. K. Grasett. (London School of Weaving.)

Useful Plants. Sowerby.

Växtfärgning for Skansk Könstvävnad. Ebba Billing.

Vegetable Dyes. E. Mairet. (Faber & Faber, 1939.)

Ver à Soie du Ricin. E. W. Adair.

Woad Plant and Its Dye. J. B. Hurry. (Oxford Press.)

Index